About the Author

Julie Marie was born in 1946 in Far Rockaway, New York, and now resides in the California coastal city of Oceanside 4.

Webs and Irises

Julie Marie

Webs and Irises

Vanguard Press

VANGUARD PAPERBACK

© Copyright 2024 **Julie Marie**
Cover design by Dorte Christjansen

The right of Julie Marie to be identified as author of
this work has been asserted by them in accordance with the
Copyright, Designs and Patents Act 1988.

All Rights Reserved

No reproduction, copy or transmission of this publication
may be made without written permission.
No paragraph of this publication may be reproduced,
copied or transmitted save with the written permission of the
publisher, or in accordance with the provisions
of the Copyright Act 1956 (as amended).

Any person who commits any unauthorised act in relation to
this publication may be liable to criminal
prosecution and civil claims for damages.

A CIP catalogue record for this title is
available from the British Library.

ISBN 978 1 80016 926 5

This is a work of fiction. Names, characters, businesses, places, events and
incidents are either the product of the author's imagination or used in a
fictitious manner. Any resemblance to actual persons, living or dead, or
actual events is purely coincidental.

Vanguard Press is an imprint of
Pegasus Elliot Mackenzie Publishers Ltd.
www.pegasuspublishers.com

First Published in 2024

Vanguard Press
Sheraton House Castle Park
Cambridge England

Printed & Bound in Great Britain

Dedication

For my sons, Demian and Blake

My sisters

And my grandchildren

A wisteria branch
Among the others
Is reaching out in midair
And not able to hold on to anything
It forms a circle
And holds onto itself.

The spider spins her webs
Web after web
Till she grows old
And spins one last time
A silken nest
In a dark corner
And then she rests
Over it
Or sometimes nearby
Till she leaves the nest
For good
And not long after
Thousands of baby spiders
Emerge from the nest
No larger than the head of a pin
Color of sunflowers
On strands of silk
Out the window
Carried by the wind
They become airborne
Across the sky
And just maybe one of them
Will land in your garden
And not pass you by.

He was hooded
Face unseen
Disturbing to look at
Like a figure from *The Walking Dead*
Mental illness?
Could be
Loss of family and finances?
Could be
Addiction?
Could be
My responsibility?
Could be.

Alice

Who would have ever thought
That you'd be spending your days
In this nursing home?
Where bed sheets are frequently changed
And the same Mozart cassettes
From a distant son
Are played over and over again
Victim of a stroke
In your bed do you lie
Surrounded by remnants of your past
Curled up and immobilized
Like the springs of a fine pocket watch
That has been over-wound.

In the lower center
Of a black-eyed Susan
A bee
Did lie without a sound
Setting in its own sun
As the other sun
Was going down.

The caretaker
Wasn't there when he should have been
And someone dropped
The stained glass window
Now shattered
Into zigzagged pieces of glass
The archangel's wings no longer golden
Mother Mary without her blue
The robes of the saints
No longer brilliant
The sheep without their hue
Do lie
In pieces on the church floor
Next to the little girl
With the pretty face
As she sits on the wooden pew
And patiently waits
For the altar boy to light the candles
And for the mass to start.

At a red light
In my rearview mirror
A homeless man
Slowly rises out of nowhere
Onto the sidewalk
And with a mass of nasturtiums
Climbing and burning beneath him
He starts his day.

Spin the webs, spin the webs
Around my head
And through my heart
Till I can see
Only a ray of light
To carry on
As a functional being
For my mate is now broken
At the seams
And this time
Isn't coming back to me.

Mr. O's Letter to his Landlord

Dear Mr. P,

"I beg you not to discard my Nike pants and shoes. I agree that that clothing
Has seen better days, but I am very fond of them. With respect to the carpet
Being cleaned in my room, I've made my mind up that being asked to pay for
Professional cleaners is unfair. This is the first accident that happened in my
Room, and it could happen to anyone. However, I am willing to negotiate.
My car will be allowed to park in the carport in exchange for professional
Carpet cleaning in my room. I apologize for the accident and let me say,
A house divided, cannot stand."

Sincerely, Mr. O

Mr. O

I'm on night watch with you
Sitting by your side
With only a lopsided lamp shade
To guide me in my writing
You have no family
No pictures hang from your walls
Only piles of National Geographics
Lie neatly in your closet
Were they your only friends?
I step outside
And walk beneath a magnolia tree's fallen leaves
Like you
Now dried by the sun and brittle
They crunch like paper seashells
As I walk over them.

The Crow

As I exit the freeway
I see you there
Against the concrete divider
You raise your uninjured wing
Fanning it ferociously
Doing the same for me
And the car behind me.

Wounded warrior
Black beauty
Most intelligent of the birds
What happened to you?

When things become humdrum
You steal our shiny objects
And carry them to your nests
At twilight you fly in groups across the sky
And when one of you dies
You gather together and mourn your loss.

Wounded warrior
Black beauty

Most intelligent of the birds
What happened to you?

I pass you again the following day
And you are still there
In the same spot
Leaning against the concrete
But not moving.

And some days later,
I pass you again
You must have attempted to escape
For your carcass lies on the asphalt
Flattened by the cars
With just a few of your oiled feathers
Caught shining in the sun.

Wounded warrior
Black beauty
Most intelligent of the birds
What happened to you?

It was raining outside
When the young girl entered the church
And sat quietly on the wooden pew
A heavy grayness permeated throughout
Draining the glass windows of their colors
Her eyes were drawn to the far-right side of the altar
Where a statue of Mary with open arms stood
Beneath Mary,
The offertory candles
Gently burned
As the women knelt and prayed.

The women light their candles
And bow their covered heads
What they are asking
For thousands of years
Has all been said,
Has all been said.

Bring my son home safely to me
Forgive my infidelity
Take away the pain from my knees
Send more money to me.

The women light their candles
And bow their covered heads

What they are asking
For thousands of years
Has all been said,
Has all been said.

Bring the rains for our crops
Forgive me for those I have forgot
Help me sleep at night
And may I no longer fight
With those in my life.

The girl didn't understand their silent prayers
For she had nothing to ask for
Yet, while sitting on the wooden pew
Behind them
A calm and peacefulness surrounded her.

The women light their candles
And bow their covered heads
What they are asking
For thousands of years
Has all been said,
Has all been said.

All of the people
Waiting for the bus
Had their heads turned
Toward the direction
From which the bus was coming
Except for one woman
Who sat in the center
Looking straight ahead.

A gentle rain and wind
Move the
Trumpet flowers
Without a sound
As a mockingbird sings to another
And the other resounds.

Gwendolyn

I had a dream about you last night
You were radiant and sensual
Your sassy self
Wearing a red dress
Waiting for your husband to return
After such a long battle
With all of your illnesses
Your house was festive
And your garden was full of
Pink and purple pinwheel flowers
All spinning simultaneously
Your face wasn't swollen
And you no longer had that look in your eyes
Of one who has fallen from their nest.

At sunset
The spiders appear
Renting their airspace
For just one night
So that they can go on with
Spinning their cartwheels
Every which way
In the garden.

As you lay in the hospital bed
In the emergency room
I pour my heart out to you
And you listen
Unable to walk away
No more rides in the old Lincolns
No more rumble seats
No more screens to put up
In the springtime
Or to take down in the fall
And no more storms to watch
Still
We are now both in a better place
Than before.

A single blade of grass
Pushes itself through the earth
And through the plastic securing the fake grass
It grows awkwardly
And stands out of place
Among its manicured counterparts.

A woman was walking through the forest
And stopped to put her hand against an oak tree
To feel its energy
And the tree spoke to her
"We, the oaks, the pines, the hickories,
And all the other trees in the forest
Stand and grow
Side by side

Though our leaves are different shapes, textures
And colors of green
When the wind blows through us, we gracefully do
A different dance
We stand and grow
Side by side

But so little is known or seen
Of our root systems that flow beneath the earth
And of how we care for and feed each other
Through the network of soil
We stand and grow
Side by side

And it is from this nourishment in our roots
That moves upward
And enters every leaf and branch

That we are able to reach the spirit sun
We stand and grow
Side by side."

The woman moved away from the tree
And continued her walk
This time looking downward
At the bases of the trees
And she smiled.

I thought that I was like a dying leaf
Held captive
By a strand of silk
From a spider's web
But I was wrong
A stranger walked by
And saw me spinning and spinning
And set me free
To fall to the ground
And start all over again.

I swam in the ocean
At sunset
And rode the waves
In the warm El Niño water
What a joy to find the sand
Sparkling, shining, and glistening
In the sink this morning!

The old woman stood
Looking outside
Alone
Vulnerable
Fragile
And empty
Like the shell of the sunflower's seed
Caught in a spider's web
Outside her window.

He was listening to his cell phone
Glued to his ear
And walked into a telephone pole
That was once a tree
With falling leaves
Now replaced with wires
Running in the shape of a T.
Do you think it was trying
To tell him something?

Roberta

Roberta had a stroke
And now lived in a nursing home
In which the floors were sterile
And everything was
Too quiet
Roberta was once a player of the game
But now she sits
In her room
Like a figurine
On a big checkerboard
Wheelchaired to her space
With foley bag in place
Among the other kings and queens
Unable to make any more moves
She waits
With no place to go.

The foghorn wails
In the middle of the night
Like a lost soul
It calls out
Only
When it can't see what's ahead
Or be seen itself.

Asphalt worn over by cars parking
Where the yellow house once stood
Souls praying in the church next door
The yellow house is gone.

Troubled girl
Trapped beneath
Not able to breathe or grow
Like the crocuses
Capsulated beneath the earth
Disturbances,
Grave disturbances
What becomes of the crocuses and daffodils
That once blossomed?
No springtime
Only struggle for years to come.

Where are these springtime flowers now?
With no sunlight to feed or nourish them
Do they crumble inside?
Into what?
Do they find a way to grow through the cement cracks?
No
Only slender blades of grass make it on that journey.

Family dispersed

False security dissipates
Father figure lost
Another dirty war.

The woman returned years later
To the remaining backyard
All that still grew beneath the fence
Were the lilies of the valley
With their still-fragrant white bells
Ringing in the wind.

The woman gently paper-cupped some
And flew them back to California

Where they died.

No longer do
The wildflowers ask
Companionship
Of the grass
They only wait
For rain to spill
So they can
Finger-paint the hills.

After he died
She dressed him
In a black suit
With a white shirt
And his favorite tie
Full of roses
Colored red
And that's how I found him
With his arms folded
Lying on the bed.

For just a moment
The sunlight captures the crow's wings
As it pivots toward the north
Like a Boeing 707
Its patent leather wings
Now shine in the sun
Then it moves on its course
Straight as an arrow
And the light is gone
And things are never the same again.

This morning on my way to work
I saw a homeless woman
Pushing her cart
And noticed
That she had taken the time
To put a white rose
In the side of her graying hair.

Celebrate the day,
Celebrate the day.

Troubled by rheumatism
The old woman
Bitterly
Walked through the town
Like a toy soldier being unwound
By the rest
Of the healthy world.

The Red-Tailed Hawk

I always look for you
While driving to work
And sometimes
I see you
Perched on top of a freeway light
Oblivious to the cars below
Rolling their rubber tires beneath you
There you sit
Over your diminished territory
Just a wedge of earth
Between the asphalt
Inspecting the earth beneath
To hunt your prey
With your mate
Sitting on another light
A distance away.

A blackbird took a bath
In a puddle of yesterday's snow
And when it had finished bathing
It flew to a birch tree branch
Then violently it shook itself
And the moment it was done
The light went out of its blue-black body
For down had gone the sun.

She lives in a board and care
Neglected
She's a little old woman
With a little face
And a little voice
And she's crying out
But I've lost her somewhere
Under all the white sheets.

Upside down
And suspended
On their webs
Do they lie
Like parachute jumpers
Waiting to be released
From the sky.

As I walk, bouquets of crepe myrtles
Fall beneath my feet
And looking up
I see my shadow moving
Ahead of me
And my shadow asks
"Where have you been?"
"I've been too busy to follow you."
"Why?" Asks the shadow
"When you were a child
You would fantasize with me
Making figures with your hands
Of animals and other shapes
And dance joyfully with me.
What happened?"
"I have been too responsible with life."
My shadow then moves behind me
A surreal image of myself
Immersed in a Payne's gray
The eyes not seen
Then I ask of my shadow
"What is your substance?"
And the shadow answers
"We depend on light to exist
The sunlight brings the most energy to your image
As other lights are not as forceful

Outside of your sphere."
And nothing more is said.

I planted seeds in my mother's garden
Fourteen came up
And I built a barricade
To protect them from the gardener
Who couldn't see
Their immature greenness
Among the full-faced roses' stems.

Bruce

My sister and I entered the mortuary's
Dimly lit, narrow hallway
Leading to your room
I didn't want you to be left alone
The night before the service
So my sister
Kept night watch with you
The gladioli fan themselves around you
In pinks, purples, whites and yellows
They interplay with the candlelight
Softening your colorless body
With your hands so neatly crossed
And holding a single purple flower
That I had picked from my garden
Bipolar victim
Intertwined to the point of excruciating pain
You took your own life away
By the Sacramento River
With a letter in the next day's mail
Telling me where to find your body
So carefully planned
Yet how difficult it must have been

To write to me
Your pain has now ended
And mine has just begun
What a shame it had to happen
The way it did
And what a price to pay
From both sides of the fence.

Tonight
There's just
A sliver of a new moon
On my horizon.

It's only in the winter
When the trees stand barren
And the birds no longer sing
That you'll find their nests
That were carefully built
And tucked away last spring.

Who will tend my garden
When I am gone?